Marri...
Conven... ♡ S0-CDN-758
        Special Events
Bill & Donna Singer
    March, 1977

Song of Love

Mike Gemme

VICTOR BOOKS

a division of SP Publications, Inc.
WHEATON, ILLINOIS 60187

Scripture quotations are from the King James Version or are the author's own paraphrase.

The author wishes to express special thanks to Edna Palmer and Treva Ward for their labor of love in typing the manuscript and to Gordon and Marie Cooney for their kindness in providing a place of solitude where the work could find its completion. With deepest appreciation, he also thanks Lois Mackey, whose loving encouragement, vision, and inspiration provided incentive to press on.

Library of Congress Catalog Card Number: 75-17169
ISBN: 0-88207-806-2

VICTOR BOOKS
A division of SP Publications, Inc.
P.O. Box 1825 • Wheaton, Ill. 60187

To Becky

The precious wife of my youth, who through love, in life, opened and filled my heart with love of God; and who through love, in death, brought my heart into the very presence of Jesus Christ.

I Love Her So

Contents

Prologue

Some men and women settle for an average married life: a normal existence of quarrels and fights, of average love, of necessity rather than pleasure. Yet for a few couples, who find real love, God's love, there is hidden within the framework of marriage the all-consuming song of love, a love which permeates every area of one's being and existence. This is the type of love portrayed in the biblical Song of Solomon.

This book takes you into the hearts and lives of two people very much in love. It is not intended to be a doctrinal interpretation. Transcending the cultures and differences in time and social strata, it delves into the hearts behind the words spoken.

This is not to be taken as a translation or even a paraphrase of the biblical book. The author takes the hearts of two lovers, Solomon and his bride, and translates their expression of love into an expression most meaningful to him.

God's love is the same regardless of generations. Solomon experienced it in his generation long ago and I can experience it in this generation of the 20th Century. This is not just any kind of love; this is love which breaks the bonds of time and space and lifts two people into the presence of God.

For the validity of my views on love I cleave to the New Testament teaching concerning God's love for man and Christ's love for His Church. These supernatural realities are to be seen in the structure of marriage (Eph. 5:22-33). No wonder people decline to believe in God on the basis of what they see in many marriages today.

Can modern-day man find profound and true love? I offer this book as a partial answer to the who, what, when, where, and why of marriage. It deals with the plan, purpose, perspective, picture, and providence of those who touch love's unbelievable reality.

This is not a story. It is a series of circumstances, thoughts, and attitudes within the framework of marriage. It may appear broken and incongruous if viewed through the eyes of story form. From beginning to end, you will read a conglomeration of loving experiences, words, feelings, and ideas that are communicated and exchanged between lovers.

It is not the kind of book that can be read and shelved in one night. Its purpose is to develop loving attitudes and practical expressions of love, to destroy discouragement, and to bring back to marriage the dignity and vision it had in the Garden of Eden.

My Heart's Deepest Longing Is for Love

The reason I proclaim these words with such confidence is that I have both seen and experienced the love of God in my heart.

I shall not spend an entire lifetime wondering or complaining because of disappointments and all of the corruption in the world around me; I shall stand tall and sing the song of love toward my precious wife. Though the world shall turn to ashes overnight, in no way shall my love for her alter or fail. I will settle for nothing less than God's perfect love for my life as well as for my most prized relationship, our marriage. I have no greater aspirations. My heart's deepest longing is toward that end.

I yield all I am, all I do, all of my rights, and, at last, my very life to experience all a man and woman can experience in the bonds of love and marriage. My mind is single, my heart is pure, and my longing is continual, night and day; for the love my blessed wife and I share is the very love of God Himself. I laid all that I am at the foot of the throne of God so He might pour into my life His love. And now I am sure that God's great desire is to flood a heart, a body, a man, a woman, and their relationship with His love.

This is my song; the song of love's fulfillment through the hearts of two people, who give themselves to each other in the bonds of marriage.

She speaks

> *"Let him kiss me with the kisses of his mouth. For thy love is better than wine"* *(Song 1:2).*

His Kisses Are More Than Just Kisses

Oh, how glad I am that he is my husband and I am the love and companion of all his days. I desire to be the nucleus of his affections and tender feelings. I desire to be in his presence and reap all the joy and blessing that is there. I want to be one in spirit with him, one in thought with him, and one in heart with him. His presence with me is the delight of my soul.

Still, with all we share together and are to one another, the delight of my life is his kiss. When a day passes that my lips do not meet his, that day misses a treasure that can never be replaced. If our marriage is apparently perfect, and he does not kiss my lips, something is gravely wrong. A kiss is the seed of affection and the first thing to suffer loss in time of dissension.

At times when my husband kisses me, I lose all of my cares in the moment of our embrace and am lifted into the heavens on the billows of his love. His kiss is not just a kiss to me—it is so much more. It is a time when our wills are united and our hearts are one; it is a moment when I can express my love in a way that words never do.

There are times when he kisses my lips with singleness of heart and mind, a time when the busy thoughts of the day can be laid aside and for but a moment we tell each other that every cell in our bodies loves more than words can describe.

In all of his sweet pecks of affection and love throughout the day, he has become sensitive to my innermost needs. I need to know and hear of his love for me. I must know that I always hold his affection. A kiss from his lips to mine is confirmation that his love is sure and strong. His kisses ring the words "I love you" in my ears the whole day long.

A kiss is not just a kiss—it is more!

> *"Look not upon me, because I am black, because the sun hath looked upon me. My mother's children were angry with me; they made me the keeper of the vineyards, but mine own vineyard have I not kept"* *(Song 1:6).*

How Can I Be His Perfect Lover?

Love is a very humbling thing. It comes to us even though, in the innocence of our hearts, we may have little conception of its full meaning. I don't think I shall ever get over my feelings of unworthiness of such an experience. With so many women in the world, why me?

I suffer many strange things as a result. The looks of some women are those of contempt and anger. Jealousy and resentments cause them to go to extremes to find fault with me, trying to spoil the evidence of love in my heart. In their personal frustration, they strive to cause me to stumble and are continuously trying to sidetrack me from my all-consuming purpose of loving my worthy husband.

My personal weakness and inability to be the perfect kind of lover for my husband is ever before me. I know, even without the pointers of my critics, that I fall far short of being that ultimate lover; yet this causes my heart to look above and beyond the forces and methods of this world for guidance and help from the Author of love Himself—God. With His presence in my heart, my capability for love is unlimited.

11

I am far from perfect, yet love is the perfection of my person to the one I love—my husband.

> *"While the king sitteth at his table, my spikenard sendeth forth the fragrance thereof"* *(Song 1:12).*

We Find Many Ways to Say, "I Love You!"

Whether my love and I are together or apart, our love for each other remains the same. This love we share is a deep love, as full in the chamber of our romance as in the light of the public eye. Our love never changes with our surroundings; it is full and real. Though the love never alters or wavers, every day we find new ways of conveying our love, which is constantly broadening and finding greater expression.

When first we married, we had a very limited frame of mind as to how we could express our love to and for each other. Now, a warm look, a gentle kiss, some loving words, a thoughtful note, and innumerable other little ways of saying "I love you" fill our hearts and minds every day.

Truly, we are enjoying the profound simplicity of our marriage. This is because each of our hearts has found "love's security" and the tenderness that it always holds toward its object. We no longer have to

12

prove anything to others or ourselves; nor do we have to feed a worldly prideful ego. We have found the rest of real love and the peace that comes from two hearts silently shouting night and day the speechless but so expressive language of love.

Consequently, wherever we go we are the ambassadors of love, carrying its fragrance and one another's presence to those with whom we come in contact. That is why I can say so confidently, "While the king sits at his table, the fragrance of my presence is there also."

"A bundle of myrrh is my well-beloved unto me; he shall lie all night between my breasts" (Song 1:13).

He Makes Me Feel Like a Queen

My husband is a bundle of love, made perfect through his never-changing devotion to the calling of love. There is never an attitude on his part that he is some kind of superman or self-sacrificing martyr for the cause of love. He is a real man and a very sincere mate. He has many faults, as every human does; still his commitment to the standard of love and intimacy seems to make any weakness insignificant.

His love for me covers a vast territory and sees the

13

desert as well as the mountain streams of refreshment. Still, in all that we experience together, his love never alters or diminishes. Sometimes I can't get over how his love is constantly growing for me, in spite of all that I am and do. He truly is a man among men. He is always my well-beloved, my bridegroom-lover, the man who holds all of my affections in a most sacred way. He knows me and loves me! I have never seen, nor will I ever see, a man who has a heart so full of the kind of love that makes me feel like a queen among women.

There are those nights when my heart is overflowing with love for him, and long after his feelings and excitement have subsided, my affections still are full. My longings cannot be put into words, so I lay his head upon my breasts and desire that he know my every heartbeat is only for him. What in words I cannot express, holding him close to the warmth of my heart for an evening of rest, seems to satisfy my veiled longing to tell him how deeply I love him.

"Behold, thou art fair, my beloved, yea, pleasant; also our bed is green" (Song 1:16).

We Make Time for Love

O my husband, I love you so much. I long to be everything you could dream of in a woman. I desire to ravish your heart with the love of my life. When I think of you my heart is filled with nothing less than love, praise, and admiration. You are always my beloved—my dearest love.

I'm so thankful that time does not rob us of the sweet gentleness we express for one another in the room of our love, upon the bed of our affections. Our bed retains the fresh harvest of love's fruitfulness, every time we yield to its warm cry. Our hearts and lives are mutually satisfied as time allows for maturity in our romance. Our bed is eternally green in the perfect season of love. And because our bed is green, each time we lie on it, the love we experience never grows old or stale; it just becomes fuller and more satisfying, as patience and time teach us how to bring our love to each other.

We find abundant satisfaction in knowing that our acceptance of each other's expression is the fullest we can know. Our feelings vary, but our hearts are always thankful for the precious evenings when our affection flows fully and freely. This physical expression continually yields the fruits of uniqueness and glad contentment.

If I were to give advice to a bride, I would tell her to keep the color tones of her room soft and its appearance neat and tidy, for in so doing she always promotes an atmosphere of fresh and eager love, awaiting only the presence of two warm and loving hearts.

Together we enjoy a love that is new and fulfilling every day, because the call of our bed is the fresh, sweet aroma of intimacy and understanding.

"The beams of our house are cedar, and our rafters of fir" (Song 1:17).

I Feel Secure in His Love

O my adoring husband, what a lover and true man he is. I do not even have a thought of any other man, for there is none to be found. There is only one man in the whole world and he is mine!

He is a man of tenderness and consideration—a man of real love. He knows my heart, reads my mind, and considers my moods. He adores our bed as much as I do, and there is no selfishness found in that intimate place. When he loves, his heart is mine and mine is his. When we lie communicating into the wee hours of the morning the unspoken words of the former day, his affection, compassion, and understanding are always toward me first.

In the secret chamber and upon our bed, we talk, we laugh, we cry, we kiss and love, we share and hug, we pray and ventilate thoughts and feelings in a beautiful harmony of oneness and intimate friendship. And sometimes deep into the twilight hours we lie beside each other holding hands, very contented and satisfied in one another's presence. We cast our eyes toward our moonlit ceiling and notice the strong beams under which the love of our lives and home abides. There is peace and love in our home, because its strong woodwork is hewn from the forest of God's love.

"I am the rose of Sharon, and the lily of the valleys" (Song 2:1).

I Am Supremely Important to Him

I am a woman. I feel like such a very special woman, because my loving husband always makes me feel excitingly feminine. His words of love and kindness, his never-ending voice of compliment and admiration, all promote the belief within my heart that I am not only special, but that I am capturing all the love one man can have and give toward one woman.

For me to know, from the lips of his mouth and the fervent overflow of his heart that I am his, breeds within me a flame of love that burns night and day.

My needs and feelings are always his foremost concern in our home. He has a listening ear, a watchful eye, and a compassionate spirit. Our home is a place of mutual labor and concern. Even at the close of the day, he does not settle to rest until he knows that I can rest also. His hand of help extends into every room in which he perceives a need.

Whether in public or private, I always sense both my supreme importance to him and his never-ending, never-wavering love and desire toward me—his Rose of Sharon and Lily of the Valley.

"He brought me to the banqueting house, and his banner over me was love" (Song 2:4).

He Tells the World He Loves Me

I feel like a queen of queens, for I hold the sincerest affections of my husband. Whenever he takes me anywhere, to dine or relax, whatever the occasion, I am assured that his attention will be focused upon me. His love fills my heart with quiet assurance that he truly cares for me.

Within our home my husband expresses his love in hundreds of little ways, but in public he raises his banner of love over me and proudly acknowledges my presence. He never fails to grasp my hand, or seat me close to him; his desire is to be close to me all the time. He never fails to turn and look at me to see if "all is well." Never has he been embarrassed or ashamed of me. "Nor will I ever!" shouts his heart of love.

Is it any wonder I love him so? He is such a manly man. He flies his banner of love over me to let the world know that I am his love and his vessel to be filled with constant affection.

> *"Take us the foxes, the little foxes, that spoil the vines; for our vines have tender grapes"* (Song 2:15).

Let Us Keep Open Hearts

My sweet wife, though the love we know is freely ours, it is naive to think that love may be maintained at small cost. We must always be aware of the forces that gather against us. Love is the greatest treasure in life, and is therefore the constant pursuit of every predator who conspires to spoil it. We must never allow the cunning foxes of irritability, selfishness, or other petty difficulties to plunder the tender fruit of love's vineyard. We must commit ourselves to a lifetime of trapping the little foxes in the snare of our love.

We must not only look at our love long range, but we must consider the fruit and its value each day!

Our feelings and experiences differ in the course of a day, and when we meet each evening we must air what is upon our hearts. Our impressions and reactions then directly affect the depth of love we can experience that evening—and in a lifetime. The foxes of quick words, snappy answers, and harsh phrases will spoil our love. These seemingly insignificant hidden foxes must be brought to the light of our love and put away.

Consequently, I always come home with a spongy heart filled with love in readiness to help, listen,

19

absorb any difficulty, or encourage in any way I possibly can. If one of these crafty foxes of enmity is left unhindered, he plunders the fruit of our love that evening and damages love's vine by destroying its tender sprouts of communication and affection—leaving only hurt feelings and cold hearts.

The fulfillment and mutual satisfaction of being together hinges on keeping an open heart to each other. Open, letting the foul odors of malice escape and allowing the fresh fragrance of our blossoming love to circulate throughout our bodies, minds, and spirits.

May we ever chase away with a perfect hatred every fox of sin that could make his home in the fertile soil of our love. May we ever be mindful of those foxes that desire to penetrate our vineyard and spoil its maturing fruit.

> *"Thy neck is like the tower of David, builded for an armory, whereon hang a thousand bucklers, all shields of mighty men" (Song 4:4).*

Your Love—What It Does to Me!

My wife, my tower of love, my heart cries out trying to describe how I feel about you. Your submissive will is always bent to my loving heart's desires. Your neck is the symbol of your strength in submission. Everytime I look upon your beautiful neck, all of love's years flash before my eyes, years filled with moments of unison and harmony within our home because of your determination to be the submissive wife you were created to be.

As time has proven, the way to a full and glorious love is cleaving to life's basic principles. I admire you because no matter how complex your surroundings become, you retain your simple heart and warm love. You build an armory of defenses to combat the natural instincts of pride, selfishness, and independence. Your life is a tower that reaches up into the sky for all those around to see the truth of loving humility and womanly honor. Where do I begin to speak of what such love does to a man's heart; all I can tell you is that I love you more than anything in the entire world.

If all of today's actions will be tomorrow's memories, I will ever be filled with the fullness of your love in my mind's storehouse!

Abiding in the depths of your love . . .

> *"Thy two breasts are like two young roes that are twins, which feed among the lilies"* *(Song 4:5).*

I Am a Prisoner of Love

My enchanting wife, my loving Roe ravishing my heart, I love you so much! Your love has been the nourishment of my heart over the years. My heart never needs ponder further than you, for you fill my life and soul with love's contentment. My love constrains me to speak of your love and how it satisfies my every longing. Your life and love ravish my total man.

It seems you are an army of love conquering every stronghold of my mind, emotions, and will. I find myself thinking night and day about your love; my emotions never rally except in your presence and the ravish of your embrace. My will submits to battalions of delightful memories and your charming and fulfilling temperament.

I have such a difficult time trying to describe how ravished my heart is by the meadow of your emotions —those two tender and soft roes, which fill my heart with unique contentment. They are an extension of your heart bringing holiness and sacred definition to my understanding. They are a part of your being which you give to fill my heart with the fragrance of your love. These lovely twins bring a ravished and fulfilled contentment to me, keeping me ever walking in the love of life—alienated from the consummate decay of lust. The warmth of your bosom inflames my soul.

From the man taken captive and held prisoner of your love.

I Love You More Than Life

My dearest love, of all that we talk about, I have never explained the secret of my unhampered love and pure affection for you. I want to now. You are perfect. You are my mind's dream.

You are perfect because that is how my love for you is. It is without conditions, boundaries, or limitations. My love for you is greater than any of your faults, stronger than your weaknesses, and more perfect than any of your flaws. Consequently, I love you unconditionally! Everything you are, do, and say is cast into my heart and reacted to by love's wonderful motivation.

I never relate to you on a one-to-one battleground or in a self-interested standoff. I cannot recall anything you have done wrong; for my love constrains me to banish all that has irritated or hurt me, to bury past wrongs in the sea of forgetfulness—never mentioned and completely forgotten.

I cannot hold a grudge in light of my heart's great desire to forgive. I cannot be impatient with you; I know that if my love is perfect toward you, it will free you to respond in love to me. I cannot be proud in "going you one better" in any conversation or disagreement, for the love in my heart detests such an overbearing manner.

My love toward you is kind and gentle, because my love has no trace of gruffness or calloused selfish affection. I can never be jealous of you, your life or activities, for my love produces a balance of wisdom,

23

gentleness, and understanding which guides me in all responding attitudes.

I can never be a worm of rudeness neglecting the respect and courtesies your womanhood and femininity deserve. All my deepest intents are those of treating, loving, and responding to your multitudinous moods and feelings with empathetic wisdom and understanding.

I never hold the gall of envy in my heart, for that would be the rancor of wickedness which would pollute my whole life. I am never happy at anything that inflicts hurt upon you in word or deed. When you are sad or experiencing any difficulty, my heart walks through the same valley with you. When you rejoice, my soul leaps upon the mountaintops with you.

I never demand the same feelings from you as I experience, especially in the chamber of our affection. In all we do and share in our life together, I hardly notice when something is done wrong or has the potential for destructive criticism. It passes by me in the flow of praise and exaltation which comes from my heart, issuing endlessly out of my mouth.

My dearest wife, I want you to know this because love is my greatest aim toward you. I hope that you will have a heart of understanding for me when I fall short of this mark. My greatest desire is to love you with every fiber of my being, and though I fall seven times seventy, I will rise again to fill your life with the love that possesses my heart!

From that man who loves you more than life.

"A garden enclosed is my sister, my spouse; a spring shut up, a fountain sealed" (Song 4:12).

I Must Drink from Your Hidden Spring of Love

How does one describe the mysterious workings and emotions of love? How do I place into words all that lies eternal within my heart for my wife?

I liken her to a beautiful piece of pottery from the Master's hand. If I love her, care for her, and cherish her, I can enhance the luster of her beauty. But my neglect or ill-will joined with hardness and lust can largely destroy any potential beauty hidden in the untouched chambers of her heart.

The greatest challenge any man can ever accept is that of bringing out the love and beauty deep within a woman's heart. The greatest rewards of sport, of physical or mental ability, or of being at the top of success' ladder cannot bring the satisfaction that comes from seeing the heart of a woman blossom under the liberty of the law of love.

A woman has no limitations in her capacity to love if a man reaches into the depths of her heart. Every woman is a fountain sealed, a spring with a lid upon it. The secret is to remove the seal which covers this treasure of the universe.

The mystery of every generation of men since time began is that of trying to bring the love of a woman's heart to the surface of her affections. How then does a man bring forth this spring, this hidden fountain, winning the total love of his wife for a lifetime?

The secret is not in the visible pool of water which is a woman's surface affections. Men have a never-ending thirst for love that is quite different from the thirst of women; that is why only a privileged few find this unbelievable love in a woman's heart. Most men are not even willing to pay the first price, which is placing a governor upon their uncontrollable, self-centered love. A man will never taste a woman's deepest love if he does not discipline his own body with the rod of patience. The abundance of love within the heart of a woman will issue forth to a man who draws it patiently and thoughtfully.

A woman has a surface pool of love, both physical and spiritual, to offer a man, whether she is a newly-wed or married 30 years. But this pool of water is not the great hidden spring within her heart; it is only her natural feeling and desire for love. The spring must be opened through time, love, and a confident trust developed in marriage.

The spring is the source of the pool; the waters seep in to keep the pool full. When a man comes along and drinks selfishly, negligent of a woman's deeper need and untapped spring of love, he drains the pool, and assumes he married the wrong person or that he has been cursed to a married life of horrible dissatisfaction.

Such a man moves out of an active relationship with his wife. Whether he physically moves out or simply disassociates himself mentally and emotionally, there is dissatisfaction and a defeatist attitude toward love. Some men run from water hole to water hole, never finding the thirst-quenching refreshment of satisfying love.

Marriage in itself is not the secret to unlocking the fountainhead of love. A few words, a pompous ceremony, and a license to drink from the pool of water as fast as a man can is not the way to gain the real love of a woman.

In many cases, marriage does little more than expose the lust-thirsty heart of a man and the inability of a woman to quench that ever-present thirst. Love is the answer, not marriage.

How, then, do a man and woman experience the fullness of complete love in every area of their relationship? A man first reckons with his motives. He must know the purpose of his efforts—to find the rich love sealed in his woman's heart.

He begins his journey by rationing the love he receives from his wife in direct proportion to her ability to give; he drinks from her pool of love, however full, ever so considerately and compassionately. He endeavors to go to the source of her love, her hidden fountain.

The only way a man finds that spring is by *giving*, in measureless proportions, out of selfless motivation, no strings attached, no conditions or bargains. As he loves unselfishly and unconditionally, he begins to dig through to that hidden spring of love. He begins to make his way through all of the distinct characteristics and mysteries of—woman!

It is under all her feelings and emotions that the pure, deep, powerful spring lies. A man delves deeper with acts of love and words of endearment. With each day and with each effort he progresses ever closer to breaking that seal upon her love. As he walks in consideration and courtesy, he begins to break through the fountainhead. He has been drinking from the surface pool to supply his needs, yet has been ever mindful of that spring of fullness which will at last gush forth in response to his gentle and long search.

A husband needs to be mindful of his task, for it

is easy to become slothful and discouraged. He must not drain all of love's available pool, because in so doing he will surely dry up what little love there may be for the future. Pure love increases the pool, but lustful cravings, without regard for a wife's feelings or needs, results in a parched pool of dried mud, filling the heart with sorrow and bitterness.

Oh, now let me tell you the glory of patience and the virtue of reticence and self-restraint. In tapping the spring of her love, you see her bloom into a flowerbed of delight to you. You see an average woman become a garden of pleasure, glory, and love to you—you alone! She responds to your unconditional love by enclosing herself into your pleasure. You have a personal and private resting place where your love and desires find unbelievable satisfaction. The more love you invest, the more love comes gushing forth from her.

Finally you shout, "How can one woman be so wonderful and loving? It must be heavenly love. I taste the very love of God Himself in loving and being loved by my remarkable wife!"

You enter the walls of love and swim in the pools of satisfaction, for your faithful love breaks the sealed fountain and the waters of love issue forth so greatly, your heart is ravished in every way!

My wife is my private garden of affections, both given and received. All th   e in my heart, no matter what form it takes, finds deepest satisfaction in her. I say confidently my wife's greatest pleasure is watching my life, filled with the fullness of her love.

> *"Sustain me with cakes of raisins, comfort me with apples; for I am sick of love"* *(Song 2:5).*

Our Nights of Romance Are Bliss

I know that my man is totally committed to being a husband and lover at all times. His love for me flows with an even tide every day of our lives. His consistence eliminated any suspicion or doubts I may have had, filling me with a desire to give my love to him.

He becomes wise in the art of opening my heart and life to his. He devotes himself to preparing my heart for our times of affection, so when the season is right, my heart is as ready as his.

He forsook the fantasies and childish ideas about love at the very onset of our marriage. He purposes to express affection that is filled with quality and satisfaction rather than one filled by selfish interest and a disarray of sexual experiences labled "love" for lack of a more descriptive name.

Some days I can sense from the very start of the day that a special time of romance is in his heart for the evening. I know his heart is waiting to be ravished in the affections of our secret chamber.

From the time he awakens, though his sweet words and special courtesies are as usual, his special look fills my heart with his desire for the evening. When he leaves for the duties of the day, his gentle hug and kiss, together with a few whispered words, make me long for the day to speed by so we can be together.

During the day, I make arrangements to see that our time will be as special and fulfilling as possible. The times flies by, and my heart rejoices in anticipation of being held in the arms of my love. There is excitement in the air of my home the entire day. My spirit wants to shout from the top of the highest mountain how much I really love him, so I patiently wait for evening to come when I can express what I cannot say in words.

When he finally arrives home, his presence fills the house and he brings me a small token to tell me how much he thought of me today. Sometimes a beautiful bouquet of flowers, or a gift which he feels expresses in a small way how much he loves me. He is forever giving to me, not just things, but rather of himself. I think at times he is almost unconscious of himself and his own needs and desires.

With all of the duties of the day met and our hearts so ripe, we retreat together to our chamber of love.

His Embrace Is Tender

Within our chamber we are alone. The affection we express is ours alone to possess. The world with all of its troubles and cares is left at the door as we enter the room of our affection. My mighty man of love knows the secret of our intimacy lies within the attitude of my mind. At this hour my thoughts are turned totally toward giving him my all.

In the tender stages of our love, his left arm proves to be a soft pillow for my lovesick head. His loving voice whispers words of beautiful melody to my heart. The embrace of his gentle arm draws my face close, to receive his soft kisses. While I am in affection's grasp on the pillow of his arm, his right hand embraces me and brings to maturity all the feelings which I have for him. My heart longs with a full desire to bring the completion of my love to him.

His heart of patience and preparation wins the victory for the expression of our love. His unselfish concern and tender affections yield the fruit of fulfillment to both of our hearts.

That man of mine is a man who walks in love's season with perfect control of all his intimate affections—what a man!

"My beloved is like a roe or a young hart; behold, he standeth behind our wall, he looketh forth at the windows, gazing through the lattice" (Song 2:9).

My Lover's Eyes Speak of Love

My husband shows love's conviction and resolution. He never allows himself to become so set in his ways, so carelessly lazy, that our love becomes stale or routine. He always strives to keep our love young and invigorating. His expressions and demeanor show forth joy and gladness whenever he is in my presence. Whether active or resting, talking or quietly sitting, his feeling toward me never changes. A soft touch, a seasoned word, a little courtesy, all convey his vital love for me.

I am valuable and important to him. He has almost a childlike simplicity in his attitude toward me. Love seems to come by him so naturally. One moment he will be exalting me before a friend; the next I will find him looking at me with a gaze that says how wonderful and precious I am to him.

I suppose there are hundreds, maybe thousands of times that he gazes at me in love and I don't even know it. He tells me that is one of his greatest treats in life, just looking at me. He says he enjoys it so much because it brings home to his heart that his love for me is not based on my performance. He sincerely loves me in spite of all that I am or do. This makes me feel most privileged among women.

"For, lo, the winter is past, the rain is over and gone" (Song 2:11).

His Love Is for All Seasons

Whatever the circumstances around us, my husband's love adapts with spontaneity, keeping me ever wondering, *How deep is his love?*

In my winters of personal distress and coldness, his love flows to me in warmth and understanding. Never is he filled with the blindness of self-pity. When my feelings and patience break on the icy shore of irritability, being in his presence, under the sunshine of his love, soon melts my icy heart of self concern. When my emotions run high and tears pour forth, his presence and love are always a soft cushion onto which my whimpering spirit falls. Whatever the season or condition of my heart, there is always a proper measure of love from the man who knows me better than anyone else in the world.

He never demands the passions of summer when my heart lingers in the place of winter's coolness. He brings me through my emotional seasons with the same understanding and love that overwhelms me every day. He is a man among men and my heart is filled with admiration and love for him!

> *"Until the day breaks and the shadows flee away, turn, my beloved, and be thou like a roe or a young hart upon the mountains of Bether" (Song 2:17).*

He Brings Me Complete Fulfillment

For all of the night my love is mine. He is mine to hold and love and kiss, and to whom to give. Sometimes into the pale hours of the morning we sup at the table of affection and drink from the well of love's conversation. Sometimes I wish that morning would never come as he turns and holds me close to the warmth of his person and I lose myself in the security and strength of his unhampered adoration.

I need his spirit of love, which communicates how much I mean to him. His well-balanced love brings fulfillment to my soul. At any hour of the night, it is never too much trouble to give him a kiss or a hug, or yield my body to his gentle touch. He is such a wise lover, and I have great respect and admiration for his gentle ways. He has won my heart through time, by being a man of consideration, having a heart full of praise and a mouth filled with kind words, thankfulness, and appreciation.

In the night season, our bed is a place where so many of my feelings and unspoken desires find richest expression. If a chill overtakes me in the cool of the night, I move close to the warmth of his person. If I need someone to share a bad dream or a burdened heart, he is always willing to sacrifice his personal comfort for my well-being. When cramps or sore muscles ache, a warm hand covers a knotted stomach or an outstretched arm bids me close that he might soothe me. If sickness strikes or illness festers in the mid of night, his loving presence is always there to comfort and help. Living with such a wonderful man—is it any wonder why I delight to be the woman who satisfies his every need?

When he turns and beckons me to his affections, is it any wonder I delight to go? He always loves me gently, patiently, and gracefully—like the beauty of a deer moving artfully across a jagged and perilous hillside. He is always aware of my frame of mind and makes provisions for the fullest and safest journey through the deepest expression and feeling of our affection. He could never force uncontrollable desires upon me.

Many nights, because I long for the closeness of his presence and need the security of his love, I bid him climb the mountain of my being and cover my form with the blanket of his presence. And how exquisite it is to have a husband whose mind is filled with concern for my needs rather than his selfish advantage.

I love him so!

> *"Open to me, my sister, my love, my dove, my undefiled; for my head is filled with dew, and my locks with drops of the night"* *(Song 5:2).*

My Desire Is Only for You

Again, my dearest love, I place the call for the fullest love to your heart. My sweet wife, love is not merely a conducting of proper motions or mechanical movements; this call is to your heart. You can give me all the symptoms of love, all the courtesies of love, and all the expressions of love; but if you withhold your heart, one day all your works and efforts will give way to hidden bitterness.

I know this is the most difficult thing I can ask of you, but it is the only way our love will last for all time. Will you open your heart to me, my dearest wife?

In giving me your heart, we begin to experience true love, not the counterfeit which is a parasite to the whims and changes of those around us. The love we exchange does not fluctuate or fall prostrate under the duress of circumstance. We are not victims of time's delusion that love is only for the newlywed or romantically gifted. Love is for all who desire it above all else. Our innermost desire is turned toward sincere and full love.

In your deep-rooted feelings you are a sister to love. Your love can flow from a place of truth and reality within your heart. Necessity and convenience are poor excuses when love can be the very rudiment of life, if you so desire. Love can be your kin and fellowship all day long.

Meditate and ruminate on the ways of love—its patience, endurance, confidence, strength, forgiveness, and all love's other manifestations to two who desire God's love and God's best. The sacrifice is great, but the treasures you possess in love's maturity will be well worth it.

Trading self-love and pride, along with self-pleasure and self-seeking is expensive to your ego, but I'm sure you find that these things only breed attitudes of bitterness, self-exaltation, and hold you in the bonds of their slavery.

My dearest love, you are free to be like a dove of peace; you can soar to heights of unparalleled fulfillment, for you know the wealth of giving and the affluence of love. Love makes you free and free indeed. Love floods your life with purity and you can no longer be defiled by selfish disappointments, discouraging depression, anxiety, fear, or worry. Within your heart you are confident that love endures to the end, carrying you into the riches of eternity.

Hate and anger, together with foolishness and bitterness, make life's routines and chores unbearable. When they rule the heart, everything you do drags in the mire of frustration and futility. As you yield to the call of love, it enriches your life and mind, making your faculties sound and sturdy. It takes time to bring your body under subjection to love; but I am patient and confident, that in due season, God's love will hold all of your life.

My spouse, I want you to open your heart to my love to the depths therein, because I wander the night seasons in prayer for you. I have no greater desire than to see you filled with unconditional love for me and those closest to you.

My prayers are not selfish, because I want to see peace prevail in your own mind and body. The greatest gift I can give you is my unconditional love, and I know that love is the only thing that will suffice your quest for meaning and purpose as a woman.

My head is filled with the dew of desire for you, and my locks drip with concern, that you have the best existence and most fulfilling experience any woman can ever have in this handbreadth of time called life.

Only love provides that.

She speaks

> *"By night on my bed I sought him whom my soul loveth. I sought him, but I found him not"* *(Song 3:1).*

When Our Love Is Wounded, I Suffer

I am a woman. There are so many complications and intricacies in my life. I am full of deep unspoken needs and unexplainable feelings and desires. Many times they make no sense to anyone around me and are misinterpreted when I attempt to verbalize them.

I desire to be heard and understood, cared for and loved, babied at times, scolded in love, hugged and kissed, supported and complimented, nurtured and encouraged.

I have a need to love and give, express and create, feel all the worthiness, fulfillment, and acceptance a woman can possibly experience. There are nights with fears of every kind that molest my tranquility and cause a restlessness and sleeplessness within me. I have perplexing feelings in the darkness of night, which only being in the presence of my husband can calm. His quiet presence, soft voice, understanding heart, and sincere prayers offer the only consolation to my disquieted spirit.

There are other occasions when my heart is worried about this special man in my life. I fear for his safety and well-being when time keeps him past his normal arrival. On such an eve, my spirit is restless and my longing heart overflows in tears and feminine fear. I wait and wait, but there is no sign of him, nor any word of his whereabouts.

I suppose I could go on all day trying to describe what it is like being a woman living in this world, but there is one thing with which my heart has a horrible time reckoning. It is those times when friction or difficulty sparks an irritation between my love and me, and we don't mend it before parting. After he leaves, my longing heart begins to yearn and gnaw away, as the moments of our separated spirits tick by. To be separated by hurt and sin is an unbearable torture that can consume my life if not remedied.

I so long to right that which is wrong and tell him of my love. My thoughts wander fearfully and my heart almost stops as I think, *What if this were our last parting—never to see one another again.* Oh, how insignificant my rage was over nothing. How foolish to speak those cutting words. My selfish pride turns to burning desire to be in his presence and tell him of my folly and love.

My soul becomes impatient for his return!

> *"Let my beloved come into his garden, and eat his pleasant fruits"* (Song 4:16).

I Am My Husband's Garden

I am my husband's. I am the garden of his love. I am his delight, the desire of his affection, the reflection of his love, and the glory of his never-ending praise. I am his.

I no longer belong to myself. I no longer have the right to live or act independently of his life and desires toward me. My body, soul, and spirit are all subservient to his "lordship of love."

How I need and long for him in every way! How I cherish his warm touch and his unselfish love!

He is a man among men! He won my heart and opened my life by enabling me to trust in him totally. I have no fears in anything I say, feel, or explain to him, for I know that he loves me and he will do nothing to hurt or harm me, either in word or deed.

I have no reservations in loving him. I know he loves me unconditionally, so I completely entrust all that I am into his hands. I put my life into his, to find meaning and purpose, by drawing my life from his. I am privileged and delighted to be the garden of my man and the pleasure of his thoughts.

Oh, let him come into his garden at the hour of his pleasure. May the embrace of my affections and kisses satisfy his heart with the fragrance of my love.

All that I am is due to the unselfish and timely love which he freely gives. The way I feel toward him, the desire of my heart to be with him, to spend time caring and cultivating his life and needs, all stem from his patience in bringing out the real woman in me.

I love him without boundaries; I feel this way toward him all my waking hours. Everything I do is within the current of bringing him pleasure and satisfaction, of having him pleased with me, having him overflow with joy as all that I am brings meaning and purpose to his life.

There are days when I long to be alone with him, separated from the hustle and bustle of everyday living, and lie beside him expressing all my heart, and he with me. What joy I have in bringing all my hidden affections to him, that he might find complete satisfaction in the garden of his delight. Again how I marvel at this man, as he is enchanted by the love we create together. His heart is always rejoicing, and his mouth carries its usual refreshment by praise and admiration.

He is forever telling me I am his bride, and the love we have for each other makes his heart sing like a bridegroom on his wedding day.

I am his garden of love. All of my orchards, flowers, and spices receive tender care at the hand of my gardener. Together we share the rapport of lovers at heart.

> *"I have put off my coat; how shall I put it on? I have washed my feet; how shall I defile them?" (Song 5:3)*

I Yield Myself to Love's Call

Again my female intricacies cause me to flounder in a sea of uncertainty. Am I sure that love is the answer to my heart's every longing? I see so much and at the same time have not seen all there is to see, and my heart stumbles at the call of such magnificent and wonderful love. Is love the answer to all of my longings? Am I capable of such grand love? What if it doesn't work for me; what if somehow I am different, and love is not the answer to my basic need? Doubts and hesitations fill my mind, as I consider the credibility of this call. The cost is great, and I am not sure I can meet such a challenge.

But wait! How long will I be pursued by this hound—the meaning and purpose of life? I feel like the prey of a thousand famished, carnivorous beasts; I feel as though love is literally eating up my entire life. How far will love carry me into its fullness? How deep will I go? How much do I want? I have so many questions!

How long will love pursue every phase of my life— barring none? I already give so much of myself; yet, can love ask and claim more? Can love claim all that I am, all my desires, all my plans and activity? Can it lay claim to every part of my heart? Is there any time I can be satisfied with selfishness or feel justified in my self-pity? Does this call of love consume every right and privilege I feel I deserve? Does it consume my vanity and pride?

Will this heavenly love destroy the vices of anger, fear, worry, impatience, and every other attitude which naturally flows from my self-centered heart? If I can truly be set free by this love, I yield to its call right now. I despise being a slave to the vices of wrath and wrong within me. Yet, why is my mind now filled with hesitation and fear?

Why? Is it because my circumstances are the only ones of their kind? Is my home and life hopeless? Am I afraid that I will be abused and hurt, that my love will be walked on and misunderstood? Am I afraid that all my most sincere efforts will go unnoticed and neglected?

Yet if this calling of love is true, then the peace of mind it affords its captors will be with me regardless of blessed or horrendous circumstances. What peace of mind and joy in heart I have in knowing that I hearken to the highest calling in life—loving my husband—there is none greater! To be at peace and know I have the promise that love will win out in the end, that love is the conquering force of the mightiest men, and that the greatest foe cannot resist its eternal strength.

What joy to my heart that love carries me into eternity and causes me to reap more eternal praise than all the glorious awards and self-efforts of mankind. To love my man is the highest calling—and I desire to follow hard after it!

"His cheeks are as a bed of spices, as sweet flowers; his lips like lilies, dropping sweet-smelling myrrh" (Song 5:13).

I Know I Am Truly Loved

Because my husband is a man of love, he suffers many times the mockery of friends, and the scorn of those who do not bear his feeling for love, who have no understanding of its makeup. Many men think my husband to be a trifling child or a "poor excuse for a man." They actually speak to his shame behind his back, because of his security in loving me and his total condemnation of lust and so-called manly pride. He refutes man's exaltation of lust in all ways, mentally, verbally, and conversationally.

Consequently, his cheeks are smitten with the accusations, harassment, and heckling of men who have no idea of the love a man and woman can experience. These are shallow types, who choose to think of themselves as some kind of "virility kings," who satisfy their fantasies by thinking they are especially attractive and the connoisseurs of love.

My husband moves far beyond those rudimental whims of pubescent self-exaltation to the deep-seated reality of love. He suffers greatly for his love; yet all those reproaches, both verbal and unspoken, reveal to me the wonderful love he possesses. His cheeks, which are smitten with criticism and folly, are a sweet-smelling fragrance of love to me.

He doesn't care for the opinions of those who beat the air with their ideas of life and love. He is the truth of love to me every day. His cheeks are like beds of fragrant spices with all the temptation and tribulation he has to endure for love's sake. His cheeks are sweet-smelling testimonies of his love and devotion to being my husband and lover. Flowers hidden in beds of honey can never produce the fragrance his cheeks of enduring love and verity do to me.

My husband is not only a wise lover; he is also able to express his love to me with perfect liberty and humility. His lips are constantly dropping the sweet scent of his never-ending love. His voice is the accent of my life. I think he could ask me to do just about anything, and I would delight to do it! In his loving tones and his knowledge of me, I have grown to trust him completely.

He never lashes out at me, nor wastes his patience in a foolish argument. His mouth imprints nothing upon the tables of my memory except love, patience, and kindness. He absorbs all my feelings and dispositions; he cools them with his patience and coats them with the balm of his understanding.

He never implies either in word, deed, or action that his life can be better or happier without me. He always conveys his deep need for me, and how I am the only one who meets the needs of his heart, and satisfies all of his dreams and desires in life. I know I am loved and needed; there is no one in this whole world who can replace me. And, oh, what that knowledge does to me!

His voice is always full of sincerity, and I know the praises that flow from his mouth are from a heart full of love—not out of necessity or obligation. In public or private, going or coming, sitting or standing, his words are tender, loving, and considerate.

He never holds his feelings within; whether they are good or bad, he finds an appropriate manner in which to convey them to me. No matter how serious a matter is, in communicating his feelings, he knits love, truth, correction, and sometimes instruction into a simple communique which expresses his heart openly. He never holds secret hurts and disappointments like a brooding child, moping for days before finally spilling forth his contrite heart.

He is always strength to my weakness, encouragement to my disenchantment, love to my faint heart, truth to any injustice, grace and forgiveness to any mistake, and in all ways he conveys his never-ending, ever-growing love for me.

> *"His legs are as pillars of marble set upon sockets of fine gold; his countenance is as Lebanon, excellent as the cedars"* (Song 5:15).

My Lover Is Strong and Compassionate

I must confess, my husband is the strength of our love. We are as much in love today as we are because he gives so much of himself, bringing love's reality to both of our hearts. His maturity, love, and understanding weave our hearts together in a single desire and vision. Our oneness brings us strength and stability that is indestructible, because of its eternal validity.

My husband knows that this relationship does not come about as a sort of "natural evolution" for every married couple. He is wise enough to know that real love comes out of humility and a total commitment. He knows that if we do not desire a close relationship, or if we are naive or casual about our love, the years do nothing but divide and separate us. So, as a wise lover, he makes provisions to see to it that nothing comes between us, by providing daily time together and a premium concern for one another's needs.

My husband is the pillar of our marriage. Because of his stability, discipline, and inner strength, we stay close to one another, and I find complete assurance and confidence in his love and trustworthiness. All I need him to be through the years—he is! I admire him so, because he outgrew his childish pleasures and independent nature even before we were married.

There is nothing that my husband would not do for me; therefore, I never fear in asking or communicating anything with him. He always tells me I am his prize! I believe it, for his life, love, and attitude show it.

He is a man who stands alone and is able to care for his own flock. He is not a sibling parasite, or a leaching burden to friends, acquaintances, or relatives!

Though he is a man of such noble strength and mighty resort, he is also a man of tears and compassion, a man who can feel my life as though it is his own. He feels my heart and understands me as much as he can; and when he can't, he accepts me in love, being available and near if I need him.

And so my heart ponders the days and months, the years and the timeless ages since man was created, and never have I found a more outstanding man than my dear husband. His life, his manner, his tenderness, and his love make him not only stand out in the generation of men, but in the very annals of time. He stands taller than the tallest cedar trees; he is deeper than the fathomless depths of any sea; he is mightier than the strongest winds and all the forces of nature.

He is the pillar of time to me; he is my spouse, my love, my man among men. Oh, how I love, honor, adore, and revere him as my lord, who loves me always and makes me soar to the highest peaks of divine love and truth.

He speaks

> "My dove, my undefiled is but one. She is the only one of her mother; she is the choice one of her who bore her. The daughters saw her, and blessed her; yea, the queens and the concubines, and they praised her" (Song 6:9).

In Praise of My Wife

Someday souls from all times and places will gather in a heavenly scene; multitudes without number shall stand before the throne of God. When God Himself beckons my wife forward to receive her reward, then, and only then, shall all men see what I know now. That woman who was "average" and generally unnoticed in the course of human events

48

will appear then as a woman of great price, honored by her Creator for fulfilling exactly that role He designed for her. It will be a surprise to all but one—me!

From the time I first met her, I knew she was a woman who would cleave for her very life to the love of God—and my love. I could see in her the two ingredients necessary for making a virtuous and godly woman: she knew, trusted, loved, and revered her Lord and heavenly Father; and she had a submissive and obedient spirit toward me. It was not put on—it was real—a part of her life.

From that time to this, she is the woman of my life, the treasure of all time to me. She always retains her purity and holds a tight watch at her heart's door. She never allows the seeds of lust or corruption to enter her life. She works diligently to keep her heart virgin and pure; she is my undefiled dove of love.

There are many virgins in this world, who may be virgins in body yet defiled and perverted within hearts and minds; victims of lustful fantasies and desires. True virginity belongs to the pure in heart, to those whose hearts are washed in the forgiving water of God's grace, regardless of any moral blunders—no matter how severe. Total forgiveness is available to any heart that desires purity. God's love flows fully and freely to the pure in heart.

Someday all shall know the truth of her deep love and shall praise her as I do now!

> *"Come, my beloved, let us go forth into the field; let us lodge in the villages"* (Song 7:11).

Our Love Is
Our Greatest Treasure

With such an overwhelming vision of love—past, present, and future—every day is filled with the delight and joy that only the reality of such love brings. My husband is such a great man, for he breaks the shackles of time and leads our hearts to the waters of eternal love. He causes me to taste the fullest love in the world, holding me close to his heart as we prepare for life in eternity, by camping in readiness of mind, heart, and spirit, while yet living on the brink of time. We are camped on the shore of time waiting for that day when we shall be carried away through death, wrapped in God's love and zeal forever.

My husband's life, love, attitude, and all he is and does reflects the reality of this truth. Wherever we go, whether good times or bad, working in fields of labor together, or standing in palace courts, we are mindful of the Source of our love and the shore where our hearts are camped in readiness. We never invested our *all* in this life; we never rooted ourselves nor ingrained our hearts negligently in life because that would cause us to lose sight of our everlasting vision.

This world is only a village to us; it is not our permanent dwelling place. We don't have to worry about building great mansions or deriving all the pleasure and substance we can from this world. We find satisfying contentment in bringing the goods and supplies of eternity into our daily lives. We shun the cheap pleasures and philosophies of "man's desperation"—we are free and free indeed!

The reality of God's love releases materialism's grip from around our hearts and minds: we draw valuable resources from hearts richly filled with the fullness of God's love. Truly, love is our greatest treasure.

> *"Let us get up early to the vineyards; let us see if the vine flourish, whether the tender grape appear, and the pomegranates bud forth. There will I give thee my love" (Song 7:12).*

Our Love Is the Morning's First Call

Each day from the first awakening, we are mindful of our love. We put down the folly of morning grumpiness—it's so selfish! Each day is met with the excitement of anticipation—to delight in our flourishing crop—*love!* There is neither wish nor reason for our affections to be withheld from one another.

Daily, it is first things first—our relationship is the first concern of each new dawn.

We enjoy spending some quiet time together in the morning, before the rest of our household awakens, to be sure "all is well" with our hearts. My husband's tenderness shows toward me from the start of the day. The morning time is a blessed time, for we break the chains of sleep early, desiring kindred spirits at the start rather than a few untimely minutes of slumber. We have great joy in the day's dawning to lift our hearts heavenward, as partakers and joint-heirs of the love of God!

We spend quiet moments in prayer, gathering spiritual manna from God's Word and humbling ourselves before one another and God to admit our weakness and inability to be the kind of husband and wife we need to be apart from His grace. Then, in faithfulness we walk lovingly toward each other, giving from hearts filled fresh with God's vitality.

Every morning differs in what it holds, and when time inhibits our quiet moments, a warm hug, a loving kiss, and a few endearing words harvest the fruitful vine, reap the tender grapes, and leave many seeds of love to be sown afresh in the planting of a new day!

> *"Oh, that thou wert as my brother, that nursed at the breasts of my mother! When I should find thee outside, I would kiss thee; yea, I would not be despised"* (Song 8:1).

Our Love Is Our All

O husband, at times I wish you were as my brother, my companion from birth. I wish all my years on earth could have been spent in your presence. I long for all my waking hours to be spent with you, to be lost in your love, to become one with your heart. I wish our childhoods could have been spent together.

At the same time, I feel as though we have always been together, that I have really known no life apart from you. You satisfy my life with the blessing of love, making my past fade into obscurity.

I love you so much—so deeply, so abundantly, so eternally. My life submissively rests in the guidelines of your love. As I look back, love was remote and foreign to my experience. All that my past contained, whether good or bad, dims and fades in the light of your love. My mistakes, as well as my fortunes of the past, my pursuits and individual achievements, lose their emotional grip as all of my attention focuses upon you.

Besides, how can I move into the fullness of your love, if I remain stagnant in personal unforgiveness and self-crucifixion, wallowing in the mire of bygone opportunities and wrong decisions. Ah, no! I left my past and follow hard after your life in love and righteous adoration.

I want you to know, my beloved, if we lived in a situation that forbade overt affection, my heart would burn with desire to touch your hand, kiss your lips, or be held close to the warmth of your body. I am never embarrassed by your tender and appropriate advances in private or public. I am never ashamed to show you my love, in our secret code, hidden to those around, but full and meaningful to us—a wink, a word, a whisper.

> *"I would lead thee, and bring thee into my mother's house, who would instruct me. I would cause thee to drink of spiced wine of the juice of my pomegranate" (Song 8:2).*

Our Romance Never Fades

There are times, my husband, when the delights of romance fill my heart, when I long to spend a quiet, relaxing, romantic evening with you. I have many ideas and suggestions from those who are older and wiser than I as to the skills of capturing a man's heart.

So I prepare an evening of solitude—just for you and me: candlelight dinner, your favorite dish, soft music, my prettiest dress, and your favorite scent. I set out to give you an evening not easily forgotten—it will give you love's hangover for the next week!

From youth into our twilight, I desire to keep our minds young with the fragrance of romance. I want you to know my heart is always growing in love for you, but never is outgrowing the delights and zeal of romance. If I live to be older than Methuselah, I never want to snuff out romance's flame. Romance and affection are two of the ingredients that give flavor to my spiced wine of love.

You are such a rewarding lover, because every extra effort I make in expressing my love to you, you notice and respond with compliments and an array of thanks. It is also charming to see how a romantic atmosphere kindles a fire within your heart. I can never foresee your outgrowing or putting down my romantic incentives.

I delight to carry your heart to love's lofty places—that defies men's imaginations!

> *"His left hand should be under my head, and his right hand should embrace me"* *(Song 8:3).*

How Favored I Am Among Women!

The normal aftermath to an evening like this usually finds us enjoying our private and affectionate embrace.

I cannot begin to describe the wise heart of my lover, my husband. His patience and self-control win my complete trust and total confidence. He is not the kind of man who only sees one course or one end in his sexual affections. He has a keen sensitivity to my feelings and desires.

He takes an evening such as this and turns it into a time of unique and complete satisfaction for both. He exercises loving self-control, while enchanting my heart with embraces he knows please the most. He often sacrifices his own pleasure to bring to me the most satisfying and rewarding time of affectionate arousal.

An evening such as this, where he sets out not to find or obtain his own satisfaction but rather to satisfy me, multiplies within me love's harvest in desire toward him. There are no conditions or secret motives involved; his only desire is to make me feel like a woman and to tell me in another way how much he adores me. His unselfish love and embrace are so obvious on such an evening. When the curtain finally draws, he tells me that his love is full and satisfied greatly in seeing my pleasure and personal satisfaction.

I lie awake, many times, hours after he descends into the chasms of sleep, thinking of how favored I am among women to have such a man—a unique husband,—who demonstrated unselfishly his love in his most intimate and loving affections toward me.

"I charge you, O daughters of Jerusalem, that ye stir not up, nor awake my love, until he please" (Song 8:4).

Our Love's Maturity Is Better Than Its Early Days

The love my dear wife and I hold for each other now makes the excitement and thrill of newlyweds appear humdrum! It takes time to grow up, to shed the cloak of self-love, to adjust to living with someone, to learn the arts and skills of being a real man and woman. Love takes time to mature! It must be weathered with great patience in the early years of development and adjustment. Some people never grow up, never emerge out of their shells of pride and self-will; they choose by action never to progress any farther than their own fantasies. Many men keep their pride rather than enjoying the bountiful harvest that comes through humility and understanding.

Oh, what a treasure there is in being a servant! A servant never has to worry about whether or not he is getting his rightful portion; he simply serves. A servant's heart is never disappointed, because everything, whether great or insignificant, is received with much thanksgiving and appreciation. Oh, to know this at the onset of marriage—when so many want to be lords and rulers.

Today, I delight in letting my wife rest and relax, to make up for some of those long candlelight evenings of labor when she works unceasingly for her family. I'm thankful my eyes are open to the true vision of love and my will is bent so I experience it.

All the love I have for my wife is not an obligation —it's an oblation!

> *"I awakened thee under the apple tree. There thy mother brought thee forth; there she brought thee forth who bore thee" (Song 8:5).*

We Were Meant to Love Each Other

Wife, you are blessed among women. No woman comes close to providing the wise love and full contentment your presence brings to my soul. I know in my heart that you and I were created for each other long before we met. We were intended for each other long before the world was made.

Our meeting and life together is not the outcome of fate; rather it is the divine plan of heaven. We were destined for each other because of the purpose and will of our heavenly Father, who nurtured, protected, matured, and directed us to one another— filling our hearts with His love. Were it not for His guiding hand, we probably would never have made it through all of our marriage adjustments and early difficulties.

But He is with us, teaching and guiding, leading us constantly forward and upward, so we may bear the image and presence of His magnificent love.

It is with unwavering assurance we know that our marriage was made in heaven, and will someday return with the harvest of love it is intended to reap.

"Set me as a seal upon thine heart, as a seal upon thine arm; for love is as strong as death; jealousy is cruel as the grave; its coals are fire which hath a most vehement flame" (Song 8:6).

Our Love Partakes of Eternity

Wife, set my love as a seal upon your heart and record that seal in the treasury of your mind. Let my love for you be sealed within your heart forever. I am astounded to think that your heart is the tabernacle—the tent of testimony—to the eternity of our love. In being such a witness your heart carries my love right through the bonds of death and into the eternal heavens.

The seal of my love, the actual love of God united with my willing spirit to love you, ties our hearts together with cords of love and the bands of affection. Your heart is forever sealed, binding and preserving all of the treasures and blessings we know together. Because your heart is eternal due to the presence of the Spirit of God, all our special feelings and affectionate sentiments, small and great, are sealed forever in the strongbox of your heart.

We always uphold love as life's greatest desire so that, if we suffer the loss of all things, even each other, our love would live on, grooming and preparing us for even greater love in eternity!

Today, my love for you grows strong and sure as do your arms, through your ceaseless labors as my wife and homemaker. As the years seal strength to your arms through diligent efforts, even so the character of our love grows strong, becoming a mighty force.

Even when you or I face the perils of the grave and the curse of death is upon us, it shall not decay or ruin the love we hold eternal for each other. Because, *our love is as strong as death!* Our love is as powerful and real as the foe of every living thing. What death is in destruction and devastation, our love is in power, righteousness, and truth! Never, no never, shall the mighty forces of woe, decay, and death ever deteriorate, wither, or in the slightest fashion impair our love.

Mighty men become weak in death's grasp, kingdoms crumble, rich men turn to beggars, strong men quake with fear, but you and I stand tall and mighty, knowing the stench of death but never feeling its sting. Death with its crashing horror and perplexing consequences is but another foe, another trial, testing the endurance and surety of our love.

> *"Many waters cannot quench love, neither can the floods drown it. If a man would give all the substance of his house for love, he would utterly be rejected"* *(Song 8:7).*

Love, the Most One Can Know in Life

You are so right, my beloved husband, we both know the security and reality of God's eternal love. I am confident that this matchless love is yours, and let me express my heart as to how vital love is to me.

Truly our love has been tried: men have ridden over our heads in abuse and criticism; we have been snared in the nets of worldliness and neglect; we have seen illness and death all around; our minds have nearly melted under the pressures of life; we have become strangers and enemies to many who rebelled against our life-style and love; we have endured hurt and distress, losses and gains; we have been through the fires of difficult times and have held our love above all else in times of affluence.

The waters of life roll over our heads and our love holds fast and increases as every day yields new purity through the refining of our hearts. God's love lifts our hearts out of the mire of average existence and carries us high above the waters of a "normal married life." We indulge in the intercourse of life and are companions in the fellowship of humility, joy, and love. Nothing has or ever will rob us of *love!*

61

We found the "Living Door" who opened to us the riches and treasures of eternity. We are so fortunate not to fall into the course of this world—that never-ending, never-satisfying cycle of momentary pleasures that only increases greedy need for wealth, success, and ownership.

We learned quickly that we could never buy another's affections. We saw how easily lust was bought and sold as a commodity of this world's so-called love. We knew God's love was going to cost more than money or materialism could ever supply. It costs self —the highest price any can pay, yet a price *all* can pay through a *total personal commitment.*

Oh, how foolish it is for men to think that money can buy everlasting love. How utterly deprived are the rich of this world, the successful, the admired possessors of many worldly goods. For in pursuing much, they have forgotten and missed the real, lasting, and enduring treasure *love.*

Blessed is the man or woman who finds God's love, whether rich or poor, homely or beautiful, brilliant or average, prince or pauper. To know real love is to possess the most one can really know and enjoy. Love utterly rejects those who pay a price less than their hearts!

We are the richest people in the world, my loving husband, for our hearts are filled with the treasures of *eternal love.*

Epilogue

You have read a commentary on the expression of God's love through two hearts. Thousands of other details and methods could have been introduced. But what you read was a real experience from the hearts of two people—my wife and me.

With your mind now filled with all the right words, proper attitudes, and whatever else you derived from this book, I wish to offer a word of caution.

You may employ all that you know and can understand about God's love and a successful marriage, you may develop a practical and workable discipline within your own heart and toward the heart of your spouse, and still utterly fail in trying to produce a beautiful marriage.

Please bear to heart that this is an expression of love, not a doctrine or method. Only one Person in the universe can fill your heart with the reality of this expression of love. Jesus Christ alone can bring the reality of God's love down into your life and home. Apart from Him, the best you can have is a pretty good imitation of the love someone else experiences.

The time has come to stop looking for the perfect words, the magical method, the most powerful enticements, and totally fall before God in our weakness and inability to love and receive from Him the unique and real expression of His love in us.

The genuine love of God comes from the heart of Jesus Christ. There is no shortcut, no get-love-quick scheme, and no perfect procedure or instant godliness. Jesus Christ is the method—He is the love and only by bringing Him into your heart, with fullest desire and submission, can you put life into your love. Love, however wonderful or perfect it may be, is doomed for an inevitable collapse if it is manufactured or copied apart from His presence in your life. Mighty or weak, rich or poor, happily married or not, we *need Him* to quicken our lives with the power and glory of His everlasting love.

It is my prayer that you will find and know this love through truly knowing and experiencing the presence of the Lord of all in your personal life.